🕮 READERS

Pre-level 1

Level 1

Level 2

A Note to Parents

DK READERS is a compelling program for beginning readers, designed in conjunction with leading literacy experts, including Dr. Linda Gambrell, Director of the Eugene T. Moore School of Education at Clemson University. Dr. Gambrell has served on the Board of Directors of the International Reading Association and as President of the National Reading Conference.

Beautiful illustrations and superb full-color photographs combine with engaging, easy-to-read stories to offer a fresh approach to each subject in the series. Each DK READER is guaranteed to capture a child's interest while developing his or her reading skills, general knowledge, and love of reading.

The five levels of DK READERS are aimed at different reading abilities, enabling you to choose the books that are exactly right for your child:

Pre-level 1 – Learning to read
Level 1   – Beginning to read
Level 2   – Beginning to read alone
Level 3   – Reading alone
Level 4   – Proficient readers

The "normal" age at which a child begins to read can be anywhere from three to eight years old, so these levels are only a general guideline.

No matter which level you select, you can be sure that you are helping your child learn to read, then read to learn!

LONDON, NEW YORK, MUNICH,
MELBOURNE, AND DELHI

Series Editor Deborah Lock
Senior Art Editor Tory Gordon-Harris
Design Assistant Sadie Thomas
U.S. Editor Elizabeth Hester
Production Claire Pearson
DTP Designer Almudena Díaz

Reading Consultant
Linda Gambrell, Ph.D.

First American Edition, 2003
03 04 05 06 07 10 9 8 7 6 5 4 3 2 1
Published in the United States by DK Publishing, Inc.
375 Hudson Street, New York, New York 10014

Published in Great Britain by Dorling Kindersley Limited

A catalog record for this book is available
from the Library of Congress

ISBN 0-7894-9992-4 -- ISBN 0-7894-9994-0 (plc)

Color reproduction by Colourscan, Singapore
Printed and bound in China by L Rex Printing Co., Ltd.

The publisher would like to thank the following for their
kind permission to reproduce their photographs:
a=above; c=center; b=below; l=left; r=right t=top;

Corbis: David Cumming 18t; David Katzenstein 22c;
Michael Keller 30-31; **Food-Pix:** Susan Marie Anderson 26-27, 32bc.
Norman Hollands: 13bcr; **Stephen Oliver:** 12bc, 15bcr.

All other images © Dorling Kindersley.
For further imformation see: www.dkimages.com

Discover more at
www.dk.com

DK READERS

Party Fun

DK Publishing, Inc.

How old are you?

invitation

crayons

Come to my

birthday party

on Saturday

at 3 p.m.

streamer

decorations

I am having
a party today.
I hang up the
decorations.

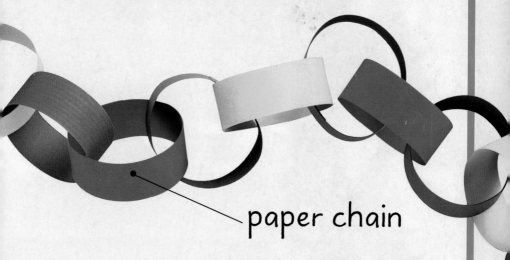

paper chain

I blow up
the balloons
and tie them
with string.

balloons

string

9

Here come
my friends in
fancy costumes.

 costumes

hat

pig ear

11

My friends give
me some presents.
What can
they be?

 presents

bow

I open the
presents.
I have some
new toys.

car

 toys

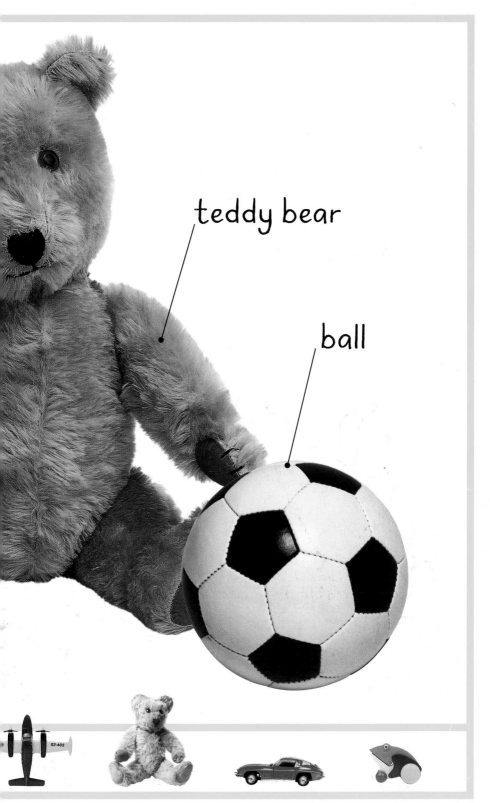

teddy bear

ball

red nose

Here comes
the clown.
He is very
funny.

clowns

16

finger puppet

The puppet show
is lots of fun.

toy box

games

We play a party
game called
hide-and-seek.

hat

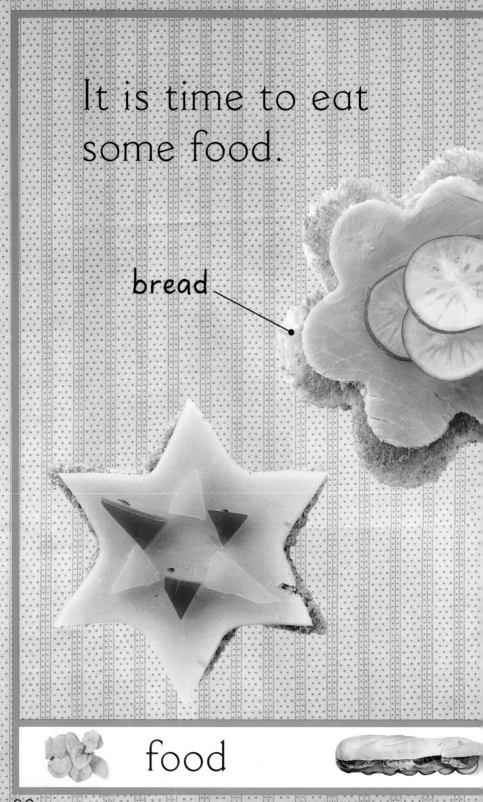

It is time to eat some food.

bread

food

cheese

I like eating
the dessert
best.

strawberry

ce cream

nuts

I blow out the candles on my cake.

candle

 cake

cake

favors

I give my
friends some
party favors.

party hat

candy

My friends say,
"Good-bye!"

When is your

birthday?

Picture word list

decoration
page 6

balloon
page 8

costume
page 10

present
page 12

toy
page 14

clown
page 16

puppet
page 18

game
page 20

food
page 22

dessert
page 24

cake
page 26

favor
page 28